Baking Cookbook

Baking Recipes that are Timeless and Easy

By
BookSumo Press

Published by
http://www.booksumo.com

ENJOY THE RECIPES?

KEEP ON COOKING
WITH 6 MORE FREE COOKBOOKS!

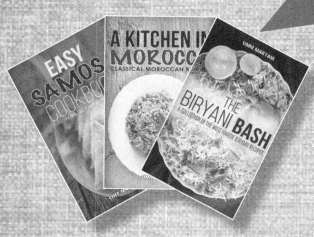

Visit our website and simply enter your email address to join the club and receive your 6 cookbooks.

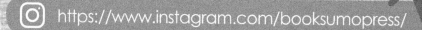

http://booksumo.com/magnet

https://www.instagram.com/booksumopress/

https://www.facebook.com/booksumo/

LEGAL NOTES

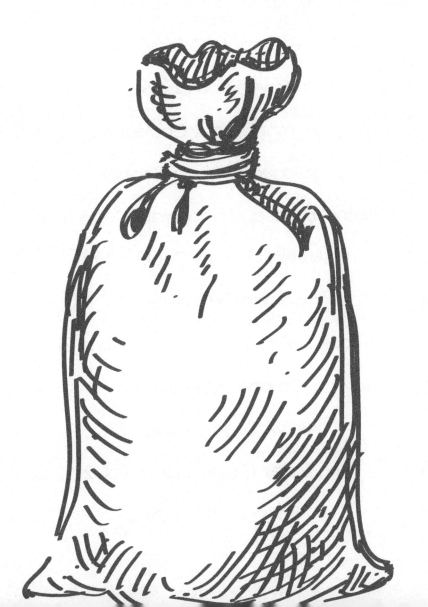

Table of Contents

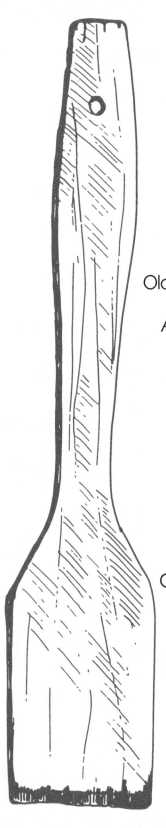

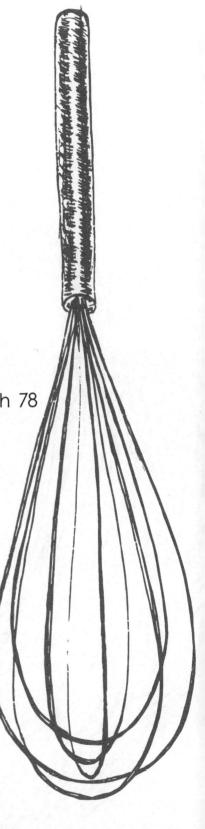

Cinnamon
Pecan Pear Bread

Prep Time: 10 mins
Total Time: 1 hr 40 mins

Servings per Recipe: 20	
Calories	279 kcal
Fat	13.1 g
Carbohydrates	38g
Protein	3.5 g
Cholesterol	28 mg
Sodium	196 mg

Ingredients

3 C. all-purpose flour
1/4 tsp baking powder
1 tsp baking soda
1 tsp salt
1 tbsp ground cinnamon
3/4 C. vegetable oil
3 eggs

2 C. white sugar
2 C. peeled shredded pears
1 C. diced pecans
2 tsps vanilla extract

Directions

1. Coat two loaf pans with oil and flour then set your oven to 325 degrees before doing anything else.
2. Get a bowl, combine: cinnamon, flour, salt, baking powder, and baking soda.
3. Get a 2nd bowl, combine: vanilla, oil, pecans, eggs, shredded pears, and sugar.
4. Now combine both bowls.
5. Pour this mix into your bread pans and cook the contents in the oven for 80 mins.
6. Let the bread lose its heat before removing it from the pan.
7. Enjoy.

OCTOBER
Ginger Cookies

Prep Time: 15 mins
Total Time: 50 mins

Servings per Recipe: 24
Calories	143 kcal
Carbohydrates	21.1 g
Cholesterol	8 mg
Fat	6 g
Protein	1.6 g
Sodium	147 mg

Ingredients

2 1/4 C. all-purpose flour
2 tsps ground ginger
1 tsp baking soda
3/4 tsp ground cinnamon
1/2 tsp ground cloves
1/4 tsp salt
3/4 C. margarine, softened

1 C. white sugar
1 egg
1 tbsp water
1/4 C. molasses
2 tbsps white sugar

Directions

1. Set your oven at 350 degrees F before doing anything else.
2. Add a mixture of flour, ginger, salt, baking soda, cloves and cinnamon into a mixture of cream, margarine, egg, molasses and water before forming small sized balls out of it and rolling them in sugar.
3. Place these balls with some distance on a baking sheet.
4. Bake everything in the preheated oven for about 10 minutes.
5. Cool it down.
6. Serve.

Country Oatmeal Cookies

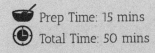

Prep Time: 15 mins
Total Time: 50 mins

Servings per Recipe: 36
Calories	144 kcal
Carbohydrates	20.6 g
Cholesterol	17 mg
Fat	6.3 g
Protein	1.9 g
Sodium	92 mg

Ingredients

1/2 C. butter, softened
1/2 C. butter flavored shortening
1 C. packed light brown sugar
1/2 C. white sugar
2 eggs
1 tsp vanilla extract
1 1/2 C. all-purpose flour

1 tsp baking soda
1 tsp ground cinnamon
1/2 tsp ground cloves
1/2 tsp salt
3 C. rolled oats
1 C. raisins

Directions

1. Set your oven at 350 degrees F before doing anything else.
2. Add a mixture of flour, cloves, cinnamon, baking soda and salt into a mixture of butter, eggs, butter flavored shortening, brown sugar, white sugar and vanilla before stirring in some oats and raisins.
3. Pour spoonfuls of this mixture with some distance on a baking sheet.
4. Bake everything in the preheated oven for about 12 minutes.
5. Cool it down.
6. Serve.

CINNAMON
Oatmeal Cookies

Prep Time: 10 mins
Total Time: 2 hrs

Servings per Recipe: 24
Calories	218 kcal
Carbohydrates	32.3 g
Cholesterol	36 mg
Fat	8.8 g
Protein	3 g
Sodium	213 mg

Ingredients

1 C. butter, softened
1 C. white sugar
1 C. packed brown sugar
2 eggs
1 tsp vanilla extract
2 C. all-purpose flour
1 tsp baking soda

1 tsp salt
1 1/2 tsps ground cinnamon
3 C. quick cooking oats

Directions

1. Set your oven at 350 degrees F before doing anything else.
2. Add a mixture of flour, salt, baking soda and cinnamon into a mixture of butter, vanilla, eggs, sugar and brown sugar before stirring in oats and forming balls out of this dough.
3. Place these balls with some distance on a baking sheet.
4. Bake everything in the preheated oven for about 10 minutes.
5. Cool it down.
6. Serve.

Canadian
Clove Cookies

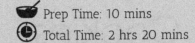 Prep Time: 10 mins
🕐 Total Time: 2 hrs 20 mins

Servings per Recipe: 24

Calories	120 kcal
Carbohydrates	18.6 g
Cholesterol	6 mg
Fat	4.7 g
Protein	1.1 g
Sodium	179 mg

Ingredients

3/4 C. margarine, melted
1 C. white sugar
1 egg
1/4 C. molasses
2 C. all-purpose flour
2 tsps baking soda
1/2 tsp salt

1 tsp ground cinnamon
1/2 tsp ground cloves
1/2 tsp ground ginger
1/2 C. white sugar

Directions

1. Set your oven at 375 degrees F before doing anything else.
2. Add a mixture of flour, ginger, salt, baking soda, cloves and cinnamon into a mixture of melted margarine, egg, molasses and sugar before forming small sized balls out of it and rolling them in sugar.
3. Place these balls with some distance on a baking sheet.
4. Bake everything in the preheated oven for about 10 minutes.
5. Cool it down.
6. Serve.

CHOCOLATE
Cookies

Prep Time: 15 mins
Total Time: 45 mins

Servings per Recipe: 60
Calories	125 kcal
Carbohydrates	15.5 g
Cholesterol	18 mg
Fat	7.1 g
Protein	1.5 g
Sodium	63 mg

Ingredients

1 C. butter, softened
1 1/2 C. white sugar
2 eggs
2 tsps vanilla extract
2 C. all-purpose flour
2/3 C. cocoa powder
3/4 tsp baking soda

1/4 tsp salt
2 C. semisweet chocolate chips
1/2 C. chopped walnuts (optional)

Directions

1. Set your oven at 350 degrees F before doing anything else.
2. Add a mixture of flour, cocoa, baking soda, and salt into a mixture of butter, sugar, eggs, and vanilla before stirring in some chocolate chips and walnuts.
3. Pour spoonfuls of this mixture with some distance on a baking sheet.
4. Bake everything in the preheated oven for about 10 minutes.
5. Cool it down.
6. Serve.

Buttery
Lemon Cookies

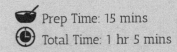 Prep Time: 15 mins

Total Time: 1 hr 5 mins

Servings per Recipe: 48	
Calories	90 kcal
Carbohydrates	12.4 g
Cholesterol	18 mg
Fat	4.1 g
Protein	1.1 g
Sodium	81 mg

Ingredients

3 C. all-purpose flour
1 tsp baking soda
1/2 tsp salt
1 C. butter, softened
1 1/2 C. white sugar
2 eggs
1/4 C. lemon juice

1 lemon, zested
1/2 tsp vanilla extract

Directions

1. Set your oven at 350 degrees F before doing anything else.
2. Add a mixture of flour, baking soda, and salt into a mixture of butter, sugar, eggs (one at a time), lemon juice, lemon zest, and vanilla extract before cooling it down for thirty minutes.
3. Pour spoonfuls of this mixture with some distance on a baking sheet.
4. Bake everything in the preheated oven for about 8 minutes.
5. Cool it down.
6. Serve.

VERMONT
Honey Cookies

Prep Time: 15 mins
Total Time: 3 hrs

Servings per Recipe: 36
Calories	284 kcal
Carbohydrates	53.9 g
Cholesterol	21 mg
Fat	6.3 g
Protein	3.7 g
Sodium	213 mg

Ingredients

1/2 C. molasses
1/4 C. honey
1/4 C. shortening
1/4 C. margarine
2 eggs
4 C. all-purpose flour
3/4 C. white sugar
1/2 C. brown sugar
1 1/2 tsps ground cardamom
1 tsp ground nutmeg

1 tsp ground cloves
1 tsp ground ginger
2 tsps anise extract
2 tsps ground cinnamon
1 1/2 tsps baking soda
1 tsp ground black pepper
1/2 tsp salt
1 C. confectioners' sugar for dusting

Directions

1. Set your oven at 350 degrees F before doing anything else.
2. Add a mixture of flour, white sugar, brown sugar, cardamom, nutmeg, cloves, ginger, anise, cinnamon, baking soda, pepper, and salt into a melted mixture of molasses, honey, shortening, eggs and margarine before forming small sized balls out of it.
3. Place these balls with some distance on a baking sheet.
4. Bake everything in the preheated oven for about 15 minutes.

Applesauce Quinoa Cookies

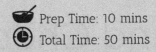 Prep Time: 10 mins

Total Time: 50 mins

Servings per Recipe: 24	
Calories	188 kcal
Carbohydrates	27.6 g
Cholesterol	0 mg
Fat	7.6 g
Protein	4.3 g
Sodium	274 mg

Ingredients

2/3 C. water
1/3 C. quinoa
1 C. shredded coconut
1 C. rolled oats
1 C. all-purpose flour
3/4 C. brown sugar
2 ripe bananas, crushed
1/2 C. applesauce
1/2 C. peanut butter
1 tsp vanilla extract

1 tsp salt
1 tsp baking soda
1 tsp baking powder
3/4 C. semisweet chocolate chips

Directions

1. Set your oven at 350 degrees F before doing anything else.
2. Bring a mixture of quinoa and water to boil, and cook for 20 minutes over medium heat.
3. Combine cooked quinoa, coconut, oats, flour, brown sugar, baking soda, crushed bananas, vanilla, applesauce, peanut butter, salt and baking powder in a large sized bowl before stirring in some chocolate chips.
4. Pour spoonfuls of this mixture with some distance on a baking sheet.
5. Bake everything in the preheated oven for about 25 minutes.
6. Cool it down.
7. Serve.

PEANUT BUTTER and Chocolate Cookies

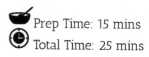

Prep Time: 15 mins
Total Time: 25 mins

Servings per Recipe: 36
Calories   207 kcal
Carbohydrates   23.7 g
Cholesterol   24 mg
Fat   12 g
Protein   3.6 g
Sodium   178 mg

Ingredients

1/2 C. butter
1/2 C. white sugar
1/3 C. packed brown sugar
1/2 C. peanut butter
1/2 tsp vanilla extract
1 egg
1 C. all-purpose flour
1 tsp baking soda
1/4 tsp salt

1/2 C. rolled oats
1 C. semisweet chocolate chips

Directions

1. Set your oven at 350 degrees F before doing anything else.
2. Add a mixture of flour, baking soda and salt into a mixture of butter, eggs, peanut butter, brown sugar, white sugar and vanilla before stirring in some oats and chocolate chips.
3. Pour spoonfuls of this mixture with some distance on a baking sheet.
4. Bake everything in the preheated oven for about 12 minutes.
5. Cool it down.
6. Serve.

Buttery
Cashew Cookies

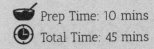 Prep Time: 10 mins
Total Time: 45 mins

Servings per Recipe: 36
Calories	162 kcal
Carbohydrates	18.3 g
Cholesterol	21 mg
Fat	9.3 g
Protein	2.1 g
Sodium	136 mg

Ingredients

1/2 C. butter, softened
1 C. brown sugar
1 egg
1/3 C. sour cream
1 tsp vanilla extract
2 C. all-purpose flour
3/4 tsp baking powder
3/4 tsp baking soda
1/4 tsp salt

1 3/4 C. chopped cashews
1/2 C. butter
3 tbsps heavy whipping cream
2 C. confectioners' sugar
1 tsp vanilla extract

Directions

1. Set your oven at 350 degrees F before doing anything else.
2. Add a mixture of flour, baking powder, baking soda and salt into a mixture of butter, egg, sour cream, white sugar and vanilla before stirring in some cashew pieces.
3. Pour spoonfuls of this mixture with some distance on a baking sheet.
4. Bake everything in the preheated oven for about 15 minutes.
5. Cool it down.
6. Now pour a melted mixture of butter, cream, confectioners' sugar and vanilla over the cookies.
7. Serve.

LEMON OIL
Cookies

Servings per Recipe: 96
Calories	72 kcal
Carbohydrates	11.4 g
Cholesterol	6 mg
Fat	2.4 g
Protein	1.1 g
Sodium	16 mg

Ingredients

2 C. milk
2 tbsps bakers' ammonia
2 1/2 C. granulated sugar
1 C. lard
1/2 tsp salt
2 eggs

1 tsp lemon oil
6 C. all-purpose flour

Directions

1. Set your oven at 350 degrees F before doing anything else and dissolve ammonia in milk.
2. Combine lemon oil, eggs, lard, sugar, flour, milk and salt before forming small sized balls out of it.
3. Place these balls with some distance on a baking sheet.
4. Bake everything in the preheated oven for about 10 minutes.
5. Cool it down.
6. Serve.

Tropical Coconut Holiday Cookies

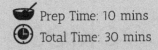 Prep Time: 10 mins

Total Time: 30 mins

Servings per Recipe: 36

Calories	154 kcal
Carbohydrates	18.4 g
Cholesterol	24 mg
Fat	8.2 g
Protein	2.5 g
Sodium	133 mg

Ingredients

2 C. all-purpose flour
1 tsp baking powder
1/2 tsp baking soda
1/2 tsp salt
1 C. butter, softened
2 C. brown sugar
2 eggs

1 tsp vanilla extract
4 C. high protein crisp rice and wheat cereal
1 C. flaked coconut
1 C. chopped walnuts
1/2 C. raisins

Directions

1. Set your oven at 375 degrees F before doing anything else.
2. Add a mixture of flour, baking powder, baking soda and salt into a mixture of butter, eggs, brown sugar and vanilla before stirring in some coconut, walnuts, cereal and raisins.
3. Pour spoonfuls of this mixture with some distance on a baking sheet.
4. Bake everything in the preheated oven for about 12 minutes.
5. Cool it down.
6. Serve.

RASPBERRY
Cookies

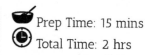

Prep Time: 15 mins
Total Time: 2 hrs

Servings per Recipe: 60
Calories	188 kcal
Carbohydrates	16.6 g
Cholesterol	37 mg
Fat	12.9 g
Protein	2.8 g
Sodium	61 mg

Ingredients

1 C. butter
1/2 C. brown sugar
2 egg yolks
2 C. all-purpose flour
2 egg whites
1 1/2 C. finely chopped walnuts

1/2 C. raspberry jam

Directions

1. Set your oven at 350 degrees F before doing anything else.
2. Stir flour into a mixture of butter, egg yolk and brown sugar and refrigerate it for at least two hours before forming small sized balls out of it and rolling them in sugar.
3. Roll these balls in egg white and then chopped walnuts.
4. Place these balls with some distance on a baking sheet and create divots with your thumb.
5. Bake everything in the preheated oven for about 15 minutes before filling that divot with raspberry jam.
6. Cool it down.
7. Serve.

Brown Sugar
Cookies

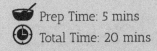 Prep Time: 5 mins
Total Time: 20 mins

Servings per Recipe: 36
Calories   164 kcal
Carbohydrates   21.6 g
Cholesterol   15 mg
Fat   7.9 g
Protein   1.6 g
Sodium   78 mg

Ingredients

1 C. shortening
1 C. brown sugar
1/2 C. white sugar
2 eggs
2 tsps vanilla extract
2 1/2 C. all-purpose flour
1 tsp baking soda

1/2 tsp salt
1 1/2 C. candy-coated chocolate pieces

Directions

1. Set your oven at 375 degrees F before doing anything else.
2. Add a mixture of flour, salt and baking soda into a mixture of cream, brown sugar, egg, white sugar and shortening before stirring in candies.
3. Pour spoonfuls of this mixture with some distance on a baking sheet.
4. Bake everything in the preheated oven for about 10 minutes.
5. Cool it down.
6. Serve.

THE EASIEST
Classical Cake Ball

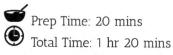

Prep Time: 20 mins
Total Time: 1 hr 20 mins

Servings per Recipe: 16
Calories	124 kcal
Carbohydrates	19.7 g
Cholesterol	< 1 mg
Fat	5.2 g
Protein	1.1 g
Sodium	143 mg

Ingredients

1 (18.25 oz.) package chocolate cake mix
1 (16 oz.) container prepared chocolate frosting

1 (3 oz.) bar chocolate flavored confectioners coating

Directions

1. Follow the package directions to cook cake mix before crumbling it into pieces and stirring in frosting.
2. Melt chocolate in microwave in a glass bowl and dip balls made from the cake mixture.
3. Put these balls on wax pepper to set until chocolate dries.
4. Serve.

Cocoa Cake Pops

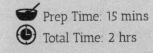 Prep Time: 15 mins

Total Time: 2 hrs

Servings per Recipe: 58
Calories	203 kcal
Carbohydrates	25.3 g
Cholesterol	19 mg
Fat	12.1 g
Protein	2.4 g
Sodium	89 mg

Ingredients

Fudge:
3/4 C. Ghirardelli unsweetened cocoa powder
2 C. all-purpose flour
1 tsp baking powder
1 tsp baking soda
1/2 tsp salt
1 3/4 C. sugar
1 C. butter or margarine, softened
2 tsps vanilla
2 large eggs
1 1/3 C. milk
Topping:
6 tbsps butter, softened

2 2/3 C. powdered sugar
1/2 C. Ghirardelli Unsweetened Cocoa
1/3 C. milk
1/2 tsp vanilla extract
Cake Pops:
5 C. Ghirardelli® 60% Cacao Bittersweet Chocolate Baking Chips
2 tbsps shortening
58 round paper lollipop or wooden craft sticks
2/3 C. Ghirardelli Classic White Baking Chips

Directions

1. Set your oven at 350 degrees F before doing anything else.
2. Add eggs (one at a time) into a mixture of cream cheese and sugar before adding vanilla.
3. Mix everything thoroughly using an electric mixer at medium high heat for about 4 minutes.
4. Pour this into a pan for baking.
5. Bake this in the preheated oven for about 35 minutes.
6. Combine some finely beaten butter and a mixture of sugar and cocoa very thoroughly before adding vanilla.
7. Now freeze balls made from a mixture of the frosting and crumbled cake for about 30 minutes. Use a tbsp to form balls and place them on some wax paper before freezing.

8. Now dip these cake pops in some melted Ghirardelli® 60% Cacao Bittersweet Chocolate Baking Chips and 1/4 tsp of the shortening and freeze it for 30 minutes before dipping it again by melting down the remaining of bittersweet chocolate and shortening.

9. When the bittersweet chocolate is set, pour melted white chocolate over these pops.

10. Refrigerate for at least an hour before serving.

11. Serve with sticks.

Pecan
Cake Ball

Prep Time: 15 mins
Total Time: 30 mins

Servings per Recipe: 8
Calories	86 kcal
Carbohydrates	8.6 g
Cholesterol	10 mg
Fat	5.5 g
Protein	0.7 g
Sodium	27 mg

Ingredients

1 C. butter, softened
1 C. confectioners' sugar
1 tsp vanilla extract
2 C. cake flour

1 C. chopped pecans
1/2 C. confectioners' sugar for rolling

Directions

1. Set your oven at 325 degrees before doing anything else.
2. Stir in cake flour and pecans into a mixture of butter, vanilla and confectioners' sugar before making inch balls out of it and placing these balls on cookie sheets.
3. Bake this in the preheated oven for about 15 minutes.
4. Cool it down and sprinkle some confectioners' sugar.
5. Serve.

YELLOW
Vanilla Cake Pop

Prep Time: 30 mins
Total Time: 2 hrs 15 mins

Servings per Recipe: 30
Calories	97 kcal
Carbohydrates	17.4 g
Cholesterol	12 mg
Fat	2.6 g
Protein	1.3 g
Sodium	36 mg

Ingredients

1 (15.25 oz.) package yellow cake mix
1 C. water
3 eggs
1/2 C. vegetable oil
1 (16 oz.) container prepared vanilla frosting
1/4 C. multicolored candy sprinkles, or

as needed(optional)
1 (24 oz.) package vanilla almond bark, or as needed
1 package paper lollipop sticks
1 12x12-inch block of Styrofoam

Directions

1. Set your oven at 350 degrees before doing anything else.
2. Combine cake mix, vegetable oil and eggs with an electric mixer at low speed for 1 minute and at high speed for 2 minutes.
3. Transfer this mixture to a baking pan.
4. Bake in the preheated oven for about 30 minutes.
5. Cool it down for 10 minutes. Crumble and mix with vanilla frosting.
6. Freeze small balls made from the mixture of crumbled cake and vanilla frosting for 15 minutes before dipping it into melted vanilla almond bark using a lollipop stick inserted in the cake pop.
7. Coat evenly.
8. Coat these cake pops with sprinkles for garnishing purposes.
9. Serve.

Cocoa
Coffee Cake Pop

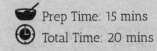 Prep Time: 15 mins

Total Time: 20 mins

Servings per Recipe: 10

Calories	123 kcal
Carbohydrates	18.4 g
Cholesterol	19 mg
Fat	5 g
Protein	2.1 g
Sodium	147 mg

Ingredients

3/4 C. all-purpose flour
1/2 C. white sugar
3 tbsps unsweetened cocoa powder
1/2 tsp baking soda
1/4 tsp baking powder
1/4 tsp salt
1/4 C. buttermilk

3 tbsps vegetable oil
1 egg
1/2 tsp vanilla extract
1/4 C. freshly brewed hot coffee

Directions

1. Combine flour, sugar, vegetable oil, cocoa, baking soda, baking powder, salt buttermilk, egg, vanilla extract using an electric mixer before stirring in coffee.

2. Fill each section of a cake pop maker with one tbsp of this mixture.

3. Bake this in a preheated oven for about 4 minutes at 350 degrees. Make sure that a toothpick inserted into the mix comes out clean.

4. Serve.

MULTICOLORED
Candy Cake Pop

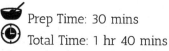

Prep Time: 30 mins
Total Time: 1 hr 40 mins

Servings per Recipe: 24
Calories	131 kcal
Carbohydrates	14.5 g
Cholesterol	4 mg
Fat	7.6 g
Protein	1.7 g
Sodium	57 mg

Ingredients

1 (12 oz.) package colored candy coating melts, divided
24 plain doughnut holes
24 lollipop sticks

1 tbsp multicolored candy sprinkles (jimmies), as desired

Directions

1. Melt down candy melts in a microwave by heating it for 30 seconds before stirring in candy coating and heating again for 30 seconds until melted.
2. Make a hole using a lollipop stick in your doughnut holes before dipping the stick in the coating and inserting it back into the hole.
3. Place everything in the refrigerator for one hour to get it firm.
4. Now dip these pops in the melted candy coating dots and sprinkle some colored candy sprinkles over it.
5. Refrigerate for another hour to give a firm look.
6. Serve.

Easy Doughnuts of Buttermilk

🥣 Prep Time: 20 mins
🕐 Total Time: 25 mins

Servings per Recipe: 36	
Calories	172 kcal
Carbohydrates	30 g
Cholesterol	18 mg
Fat	4.7 g
Protein	2.7 g
Sodium	189 mg

Ingredients

2 cups vegetable oil for frying
Doughnuts:
2 cups buttermilk
1 cup white sugar
2 large eggs, beaten
5 cups sifted all-purpose flour
2 tsps baking soda
1 tsp baking powder
1 tsp salt
1 tsp ground nutmeg

1/4 tsp ground cinnamon
1/2 cup melted butter
Glaze:
3 cups confectioners' sugar
1 tbsp margarine, softened (optional)
1/2 tsp vanilla extract
2 tbsps milk, or as needed

Directions

1. Get a deep fryer. Set oil to 375 degrees.
2. Get a bowl mix the following ingredients: eggs, buttermilk, and white sugar.
3. Get a 2nd bowl to mix: cinnamon, flour, nutmeg, baking soda, salt, and baking powder.
4. Mix both bowls with butter and form dough.
5. Add flour to a countertop for rolling the dough.
6. Roll dough to a thickness of 1/4 of an inch cut with doughnut cutter.
7. Get another bowl to make glaze: vanilla extract, sugar, and margarine. Slowly add milk to make a glaze.
8. Fry doughnuts in batches for 1 min per side.
9. Remove from oil and drain excess.
10. Cover each doughnut with glaze.
11. Enjoy.

EASY CLASSICAL
Doughnut I

 Prep Time: 10 mins

Total Time: 20 mins

Servings per Recipe: 8

Calories	366 kcal
Carbohydrates	30.1 g
Cholesterol	< 1 mg
Fat	26.8 g
Protein	2.3 g
Sodium	350 mg

Ingredients

2 quarts oil for deep frying
1 (10 ounce) can refrigerated buttermilk
biscuit dough
1 cup confectioners' sugar

Directions

1. Get a fryer set to 375 degrees F with oil in it.
2. Grab biscuit mix and take them apart. Create a hole in each biscuit.
3. Put biscuits in deep fryer. Fry until golden.
4. Remove from oil. Remove excess oils with paper towels.
5. Get a container or bag. Add sugar. Place one doughnut into the sugar. Cover and shake to coat.

Classical Doughnuts
of Applesauce I

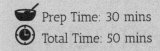 Prep Time: 30 mins
🕐 Total Time: 50 mins

Servings per Recipe: 24
Calories   190 kcal
Carbohydrates   24.7 g
Cholesterol   18 mg
Fat   9 g
Protein   2.9 g
Sodium   172 mg

Ingredients

2 quarts oil for deep frying
3/4 cup white sugar
2 tbsps butter, softened
2 eggs
3/4 cup applesauce
4 cups sifted all-purpose flour
2 tsps baking powder
1 tsp salt

1/2 tsp baking soda
1/2 tsp ground mace
1/2 tsp ground cinnamon
1/2 cup buttermilk
1/4 cup confectioners' sugar for dusting

Directions

1. Get a deep fryer. Set oil to 375 degrees.
2. Get a bowl, mix: applesauce, sugar, eggs, and butter.
3. Get 2nd bowl, mix: cinnamon, flour, mace, baking powder, baking soda, and salt
4. Combine both bowls and stir in buttermilk to make dough.
5. Add flour to a countertop for rolling out the dough.
6. Roll dough to a thickness of 1/4 of an inch. Cut with doughnut cutter.
7. Fry doughnuts in batches for 1 min per side.
8. Remove from oil and drain excess.

CLASSICAL
Herman Doughnuts I

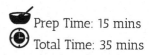

Prep Time: 15 mins
Total Time: 35 mins

Servings per Recipe: 12
Calories   289 kcal
Carbohydrates   26.1 g
Cholesterol   32 mg
Fat   19.1 g
Protein   3.5 g
Sodium   218 mg

Ingredients

8 cups vegetable oil (for frying)
3 tbsps shortening
1/2 cup white sugar
2 eggs, beaten
1 cup Herman Sourdough Starter
1/2 cup milk
2 cups all-purpose flour

1 tsp baking soda
1/2 tsp salt
1/4 tsp ground nutmeg
2 tbsps confectioners' sugar

Directions

1. Get a bowl, mix: sugar and shortening, milk and Herman starter (make a cream).
2. Get a 2nd bowl, mix: nutmeg, flour, and baking soda.
3. Combine both bowls, knead, to form dough.
4. Add flour to a countertop for rolling out the dough.
5. Roll dough to a thickness of 1/4 of an inch cut with doughnut cutter.
6. Let doughnuts sit for 1 hour while covered to rise.
7. Get a deep fryer. Set oil to 375 degrees.
8. Fry doughnuts in batches for 1 min per side.
9. Remove from oil. Drain excess. Enjoy.

Doughnuts
In Poland

Prep Time: 30 mins
Total Time: 50 mins

Servings per Recipe: 36
Calories   218 kcal
Carbohydrates   28 g
Cholesterol   30 mg
Fat   9.9 g
Protein   4 g
Sodium   54 mg

Ingredients

1 (0.6 ounce) cake compressed fresh yeast
3 tbsps warm water (110 degrees F/45 degrees C)
1 tsp white sugar
3 cups milk
3/4 cup margarine
5 egg yolks

3/4 cup white sugar
8 cups all-purpose flour
8 cups shortening for frying
1/4 cup white sugar

Directions

1. Get a bowl, mix into a paste: 1 tsp of sugar, water, and yeast. Set aside and let it rise.
2. Get a pan heat and stir milk and margarine. Set aside.
3. Get a bowl, mix until foamy: 3/4 cup of sugar and egg yolks (mix these until they are smooth first), and milk and margarine mixture.
4. Combine foamy mixture with yeast mixture while slowly adding flour, to make soft dough.
5. Let dough double in size.
6. Use dough to make as many balls as possible. Set aside and let them double in size.
7. Fry balls in 375 degree shortening until golden on all sides.
8. Let everything drain. Cover in sugar.
9. Enjoy.

DOUGHNUTS
In Canada

Prep Time: 15 mins
Total Time: 30 mins

Servings per Recipe: 36

Calories	0 mg
Carbohydrates	23.3 g
Cholesterol	0 mg
Fat	1.9 g
Protein	3.4 g
Sodium	66 mg

Ingredients

1 tbsp white sugar
1/2 cup warm water (110 degrees F/45 degrees C)
1 tbsp active dry yeast
1/4 cup vegetable oil
2 1/3 cups warm water (110 degrees F/45 degrees C)
1 tsp salt
4 tbsps white sugar

4 cups all-purpose flour
4 cups whole wheat flour
1 tbsp lemon juice
3 tbsps white sugar
1 tsp ground cinnamon

Directions

1. Get a bowl, mix: 1/2 cup of warm water, and one tbsp of yeast and sugar. Set aside.
2. Get a bowl, mix: 4 tbsps of sugar, oil, salt, 2 and 1/3 cups of water.
3. Mix everything together with yeast and flour, form dough.
4. Get another bowl, add butter, and coat dough with butter.
5. Cover container. Let dough rise for 1.5 hours.
6. Remove pieces of dough. Form egg like shapes. Flatten to make ovals.
7. Fry ovals in 350 degrees until completely golden.
8. Take out of oil and remove any excess. Coat with lemon juice, white sugar, and cinnamon.
9. Enjoy.

Super Simple
Doughnuts with Jelly

🥣 Prep Time: 30 mins
🕐 Total Time: 2 hrs 35 mins

Servings per Recipe: 24	
Calories	232 kcal
Carbohydrates	32.5 g
Cholesterol	9 mg
Fat	9.6 g
Protein	3.9 g
Sodium	124 mg

Ingredients

1 cup warm milk (110 degrees F / 45 degrees C)
1/3 cup water
1 egg, beaten
3 tbsps margarine, melted
3/4 cup white sugar
4 1/2 cups bread flour
1 tsp salt
1 1/2 tsps ground nutmeg

1 tbsp active dry yeast
3/4 cup any flavor fruit jam
2 quarts vegetable oil for frying

Directions

1. Get a bread machine, add: yeast, milk, nutmeg, beaten egg, water, salt, melted butter, bread flour, and sugar.
2. Set machine to dough setting. Let it work.
3. Place dough on a floured surface. Let it sit for 13 mins.
4. Flatten dough to a ¼ inch thick sheet.
5. Use a cutter to form 2 inch pieces.
6. Separate pieces into two sets.
7. Add half tsp of jam to half.
8. Wet the outside edge of each jam cutout with cold water and cover them with the other cutouts that do not have any jam. Pinch edges to seal.
9. Set aside and let them rise for 45 mins to 1 hour.
10. Fry in 375 degrees. Until completely golden.
11. Add some sugar coating.
12. Enjoy.

A SIMPLE
Doughnut of Yeast

Prep Time: 30 mins
Total Time: 2 hrs 45 mins

Servings per Recipe: 18

Calories	542 kcal
Carbohydrates	68.7 g
Cholesterol	57 mg
Fat	26.7 g
Protein	7.7 g
Sodium	191 mg

Ingredients

3 1/2 cups all-purpose flour
2 (.25 ounce) packages active dry yeast
3/4 cup milk
3/4 cup white sugar
1/4 cup butter
1/2 tsp salt

2 eggs
2 quarts oil for deep frying
1 cup confectioners' sugar for dusting

Directions

1. Get a bowl, mix: yeast, and 1 and 3/4 cups of flour.
2. Get a pan, heat and stir until smooth: salt, milk, butter, and sugar.
3. Combine milk and melted butter with the flour mixture, add your eggs. Mix evenly.
4. Use electric mixer on low, for 1 minute.
5. At highest setting continue mixing for 3 mins.
6. Get a spoon, add flour until dough forms.
7. Knead dough on floured surface for 4 mins.
8. Get an oiled bowl, let dough sit for 1 hr to rise.
9. Flatten dough to ½ in sheet. Use cutter to make doughnuts. Let them rise for 1 hr.
10. Get deep fryer with oil at 375 degrees. Fry doughnuts in batches until completely golden.
11. Let cool and cover with confectioner's sugar.

A Muffin
That Is A Doughnut Too

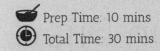 Prep Time: 10 mins

Total Time: 30 mins

Servings per Recipe: 12	
Calories	216 kcal
Carbohydrates	37.7 g
Cholesterol	16 mg
Fat	6.5 g
Protein	2.5 g
Sodium	152 mg

Ingredients

1/3 cup shortening
1 cup white sugar
1 egg
1 1/2 cups all-purpose flour
1 1/2 tsps baking powder
1/2 tsp salt

1/4 tsp ground cinnamon
1/2 cup milk
1/2 cup white sugar
1 tsp ground cinnamon

Directions

1. Set oven to 375 degrees Fahrenheit. Coat a muffin tin with oil.
2. Get a bowl, mix until creamy: 1 cup of sugar, shortening, and eggs (should be beat prior to this point).
3. Get 2nd bowl, mix: one fourth of a tsp of cinnamon, flour, salt, and baking powder.
4. Mix both with milk, make batter. Fill muffin tin with it.
5. Bake for 20 mins.
6. Get a bowl, mix: 1 tsp of cinnamon and 1/2 cup of sugar.
7. Let muffins cool. Coat with sugar and cinnamon.

ARTISAN
Sun-Dried Pesto Quiche

Prep Time: 15 mins
Total Time: 45 mins

Servings per Recipe: 8
Calories	222 kcal
Fat	16.1 g
Carbohydrates	13.1g
Protein	6.6 g
Cholesterol	81 mg
Sodium	235 mg

Ingredients

4 tbsps pesto
1 (9 in.) unbaked pie crust
4 tbsps crumbled goat cheese
3 eggs
1/2 C. half-and-half cream
1 tbsp all-purpose flour

8 oil-packed sun-dried tomatoes, drained and cut into strips
salt and freshly ground black pepper to taste

Directions

1. Coat your pie dish with pesto and goat cheese then set your oven to 400 degrees before doing anything else.
2. Get a bowl, combine: pepper, flour, salt, cream, and whisked eggs.
3. Enter this into your pie crust and then layer the sun dried tomatoes over the mix.
4. Cook the quiche in the oven for 32 mins.
5. Enjoy.

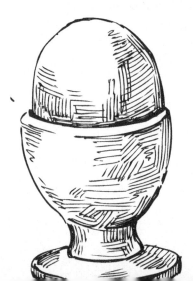

A Quiche
from Maine

Prep Time: 45 mins
Total Time: 1 hr 20 mins

Servings per Recipe: 8
Calories	154 kcal
Fat	9.3 g
Carbohydrates	6.7g
Protein	10.8 g
Cholesterol	99 mg
Sodium	289 mg

Ingredients

2 tbsps butter, divided
1/4 C. plain dried bread crumbs
2 C. 2% milk
8 oz. salmon fillets, skin removed
1/3 C. diced onion
1/2 bunch Swiss chard, diced
1/2 tsp salt
1/8 tsp ground black pepper

1/2 tsp dried marjoram
1/8 tsp ground nutmeg
3 eggs

Directions

1. Coat a pie dish with 1 tbsp of butter then set your oven to 350 degrees before doing anything else.
2. Now coat the pie dish with bread crumbs and shake off any excess.
3. Begin to simmer your salmon in milk, in a large pot with a lid.
4. Cook the salmon for 12 mins.
5. Now in a separate pan begin to stir fry your chards and onions in the rest of the butter.
6. Once all of the liquid has cooked out add: nutmeg, salt, marjoram, and pepper.
7. Remove everything from the pan and let the contents cool.
8. Enter the onion mix in to the pie dish and then flake your salmon into the mix as well.
9. Now get a bowl, combine: 1 C. of milk from the salmon and the eggs.
10. Pour this into the pie crust as well and cook everything in the oven for 40 mins.
11. Enjoy.

CHERRY TOMATOES
and Kale Quiche

🍳 Prep Time: 15 mins
🕐 Total Time: 1 hr 10 mins

Servings per Recipe: 8

Calories	110 kcal
Fat	7 g
Carbohydrates	4.1g
Protein	8 g
Cholesterol	106 mg
Sodium	217 mg

Ingredients

1 C. diced kale
1 small leek, white and light green parts only, sliced
4 oz. halved cherry tomatoes
4 eggs
1 C. milk
4 oz. shredded Italian cheese blend

1 sprig fresh rosemary, finely diced
1 pin. sea salt
1/8 tsp ground black pepper
1 tbsp grated Parmesan cheese

Directions

1. Coat a pie plate with oil and then set your oven to 375 degrees before doing anything else.
2. Steam your kale over 2 inches of boiling water, in a large pot, using a steamer insert.
3. Place a lid on the pot and let the contents cook for 7 mins. Then place the kale into the pie plate.
4. Now combine the sliced tomatoes and leeks with the kale.
5. Get a bowl, combine: black pepper, milk, sea salt, cheese, and rosemary.
6. Enter this mix into the pie plate and stir the contents.
7. Cook everything in the oven for 35 mins.
8. Now place a topping of parmesan over the quiche and continue cooking it in the oven for 15 more mins.
9. Enjoy.

Pikeville Style Biscuits

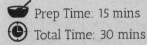 Prep Time: 15 mins
Total Time: 30 mins

Servings per Recipe: 12
Calories	154 kcal
Fat	8 g
Carbohydrates	17.9g
Protein	2.7 g
Cholesterol	21 mg
Sodium	231 mg

Ingredients

2 C. all-purpose flour
2 1/2 tsp baking powder
1/2 tsp baking soda
1 dash salt
1 tbsp white sugar

1/2 C. butter
3/4 C. buttermilk

Directions

1. Set your oven to 400 degrees F before doing anything else.
2. In a bowl, mix together the flour, baking soda, baking powder, sugar and salt.
3. With a pastry cutter, cut the butter and mix till a coarse crumb forms.
4. Add the buttermilk and mix till well combined.
5. Place the dough onto a floured surface and knead for about 2 minutes.
6. Place the dough onto a baking sheet and roll into a 6x6-inch square, then cut into 12 even sections.
7. Cook in the oven for about 15 minutes.
8. Separate into the biscuits and serve hot.

AUTUMN
Almonds

Prep Time: 15 mins
Total Time: 1 hr 15 mins

Servings per Recipe: 16
Calories	231 kcal
Fat	18 g
Carbohydrates	13.3g
Protein	7.8 g
Cholesterol	0 mg
Sodium	40 mg

Ingredients

1 egg white
1 tsp cold water
4 C. whole almonds
1/2 C. white sugar

1/4 tsp salt
1/2 tsp ground cinnamon

Directions

1. Set your oven to 250 degrees before doing anything else.
2. Get a bowl, stir: water and egg white. Work the mix until it is fluffy then stir in the nuts.
3. Now combine in the cinnamon, salt, and sugar.
4. Work the mix evenly.
5. Layer your mix on the dish and cook everything in the oven for 60 mins.
6. Place your almonds in a storage dish.
7. Enjoy.

Almonds and Figs

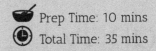 Prep Time: 10 mins

Total Time: 35 mins

Servings per Recipe: 12

Calories	187 kcal
Fat	12.3 g
Carbohydrates	12.1g
Protein	8.3 g
Cholesterol	33 mg
Sodium	211 mg

Ingredients

1/2 C. brown sugar
2 tbsps water
6 fresh figs, stemmed and quartered
1 (14 oz.) round 4 1/4-inch diameter
round Brie cheese
1/2 C. toasted almonds

1/2 tsp vanilla extract

Directions

1. Set your oven to 325 degrees before doing anything else.
2. Heat your sugar in a pan until it is melted then combine in the vanilla and figs.
3. Stir and heat everything for 12 mins then combine in the almonds and stir everything again.
4. Layer your brie into a casserole dish and top it with the vanilla mix.
5. Cook everything in the oven for 13 mins.
6. Enjoy with crackers.

EASY ALMOND
Candy I

Prep Time: 20 mins
Total Time: 1 hr

Servings per Recipe: 12
Calories	345 kcal
Fat	21.6 g
Carbohydrates	34.1g
Protein	4.9 g
Cholesterol	56 mg
Sodium	116 mg

Ingredients

1 C. butter
3/4 C. white sugar
1 egg
1/2 C. almond paste

1 tsp almond extract
2 C. all-purpose flour
2 1/2 oz. sliced almonds

Directions

1. Set your oven to 350 degrees before doing anything else.
2. Get a bowl and beat your butter in it until it is creamy then combine in the sugar slowly and continue to work the mix until it is frothy.
3. Combine in the egg yolks only and place the whites to the side.
4. Stir the mix then add in the flavoring and almond paste.
5. Continue to mix everything then add in the flour and mix everything again.
6. Layer the mix into a 13x9 baking dish and beat your egg whites until they are foamy.
7. Top the dough with the whites and cover everything with almonds.
8. Cook the dish in the oven for 40 mins.
9. Then cut everything into squares.
10. Enjoy.

Easy Almond Candy II

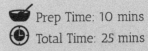 Prep Time: 10 mins
Total Time: 25 mins

Servings per Recipe: 12
Calories   147 kcal
Fat   2 g
Carbohydrates   29 g
Protein   3.1 g
Cholesterol   31 mg
Sodium   12 mg

Ingredients

1 1/2 C. all-purpose flour
1 C. white sugar
2 tsps almond extract
2 eggs

1/4 C. sliced almonds

Directions

1. Set your oven to 350 degrees before doing anything else.
2. Get a bowl, combine: sugar and flour. Then combine in the eggs and almond extract.
3. Stir everything nicely and shape the resulting dough into small balls of 1 inch.
4. Layer everything onto a baking sheet and press an almond into each one.
5. Cook everything in the oven for 12 mins.
6. Enjoy.

ITALIANO
Biscotti

Prep Time: 20 mins
Total Time: 1 hr

Servings per Recipe: 12

Calories	219 kcal
Fat	4.6 g
Carbohydrates	39.9g
Protein	4.8 g
Cholesterol	46 mg
Sodium	99 mg

Ingredients

2 1/4 C. all-purpose flour
1 1/4 C. white sugar
1 pinch salt
2 tsps baking powder
1/2 C. sliced almonds
1 tbsp orange zest

3 egg, beaten
1 tbsp vegetable oil
1/4 tsp almond extract

Directions

1. Coat a cookie sheet with oil and flour then set your oven to 350 degrees before doing anything else.
2. Get a bowl, combine: orange zest, flour, almonds, sugar, salt, and baking powder.
3. Now work in your almond extract, oil, and eggs. By hand, work the mix into a ball then break it into 2 pieces and shape each one into a cylinder.
4. Layer your cylinders onto the cookie sheets and flatten them.
5. Cook everything in the oven for 22 mins.
6. Cut the cylinders diagonally after letting them cool slightly then bake everything again for 12 more mins.
7. Enjoy.

Macaroons
3

Prep Time: 20 mins
Total Time: 40 mins

Servings per Recipe: 12	
Calories	182 kcal
Fat	6 g
Carbohydrates	30.5g
Protein	3.1 g
Cholesterol	0 mg
Sodium	40 mg

Ingredients

1/2 lb almond paste
1 C. white sugar
3 egg whites
1/8 tsp salt
2 tbsps cake flour
1/3 C. confectioners' sugar

2 tbsps chopped blanched almonds

Directions

1. Get a few baking sheets and place some parchment paper on each one.
2. Add your almond paste to a food processor and soften it.
3. Get a bowl, combine: sugar and almond paste.
4. Now separate the egg yolks and the egg whites. Combine in the salt, flour, and confectioners.
5. Press the dough through a cookie press and layer dollops of the mix onto the baking sheet.
6. Place a covering over the cookies and leave them for 35 mins.
7. Now set your oven to 300 degrees before continuing and let it get hot.
8. Top your cookies with the almonds and cook them in the oven for 30 mins.
9. Now let everything cool.

ALMOND
Brittle

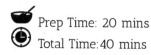

Prep Time: 20 mins
Total Time: 40 mins

Servings per Recipe: 30
Calories	176 kcal
Fat	10.2 g
Carbohydrates	21.5g
Protein	1.9 g
Cholesterol	15 mg
Sodium	33 mg

Ingredients

3/4 C. butter
2 C. white sugar
1 C. chopped almonds
2 C. milk chocolate chips

1/2 C. finely chopped almonds

Directions

1. Add the following to a pot: 1 C. almonds, butter, and sugar.
2. Whisk the mix and heat it until it is boiling then stop stirring and let it thicken.
3. Layer the mix onto a baking sheet coated with butter and press the chocolate pieces into the mix.
4. Top everything with the finely chopped almonds and once the dish is completely cool.
5. Break it into pieces.
6. Enjoy.

A Jewish Pastry (Roogala)

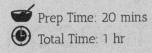

Prep Time: 20 mins
Total Time: 1 hr

Servings per Recipe: 24
Calories	136 kcal
Fat	8 g
Carbohydrates	15.1g
Protein	2.2 g
Cholesterol	23 mg
Sodium	22 mg

Ingredients

1 C. all-purpose flour
1/2 C. unsalted butter, chilled
4 oz. cream cheese, cold
3/4 C. apricot jam
1/4 C. white sugar
1/2 C. toasted and chopped almonds

1 tsp lemon zest
1 egg
1/3 C. chopped almonds
1/3 C. sifted confectioners' sugar

Directions

1. Add your flour to a bowl then cut in the butter and work the mix with either your hands or with a mixer until it becomes crumbs then cut in the cream cheese.
2. Work the mix until it becomes a dough. Shape everything into 1 ball then break the ball into two pieces.
3. Cover each piece with some plastic and put everything in the fridge.
4. Add your apricot jam to a bowl and beat it until it is soft, then add in the nuts and sugar and stir everything nicely.
5. Take out your dough from the fridge and place one on a cutting board coated with flour. Roll out the dough into a circle. And top it with the almond mix.
6. Do the same thing for the other piece of dough.
7. Slice each circle into twelve triangles then place everything onto a cookie sheet covered with parchment paper.
8. Now set your oven to 350 degrees before continuing and coat everything with some beaten eggs and more nuts.
9. Cook the cookies in the oven for 22 mins.
10. Serve after topping the cookies with some confectioner's sugar.
11. Enjoy.

OLD-FASHIONED
American Pecan Pie

Prep Time: 10 mins
Total Time: 55 mins

Servings per Recipe: 6
Calories   653.4
Fat   37.4
Cholesterol   120.0m
Sodium   282.6mg
Carbohydrates   78.3
Protein   6.9g

Ingredients

3 eggs
1 C. corn syrup
1 tsp vanilla extract
1 1/4 C. pecan halves
2/3 C. sugar

1/3 C. butter (melted)
1 pie crust

Directions

1. Set your oven to 350 degrees F before doing anything else.
2. In a bowl, add the eggs and beat lightly.
3. Add the corn syrup, sugar, butter and vanilla extract and stir to combine well.
4. Stir in the pecan halves and place the filling into crust.
5. Cover the edges with a piece of the foil and cook in the oven for about 25 minutes.
6. Remove the piece of foil and cook in the oven for about 20 minutes.

Apple Pie from the Netherlands

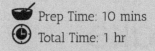

Prep Time: 10 mins
Total Time: 1 hr

Servings per Recipe: 8
Calories   405.5
Fat   15.4
Cholesterol   20.3m
Sodium   189.5mg
Carbohydrates   65.8
Protein   3.2g

Ingredients

1 ready-made pie crust
5 1/2 C. peeled cored sliced cooking apples
1 tbsp lemon juice
1/2 C. granulated sugar
1/4 C. brown sugar, packed
3 tbsp flour
1/2 tsp ground cinnamon
1/4 tsp nutmeg

Topping
3/4 C. flour
1/4 C. granulated sugar
1/4 C. brown sugar, packed
1/3 C. butter, room temperature

Directions

1. Set your oven to 375 degrees F before doing anything else.
2. Arrange the pie crust into the pie plate.
3. In a large bowl, mix together the sliced apples, lemon juice, both sugars, flour, cinnamon and nutmeg.
4. Place the apple mixture into the crust.
5. For topping in a medium bowl, add the flour, both sugars and butter and with a fork, mix till a coarse crumb mixture forms.
6. Sprinkle the crumb mixture over the apples evenly.
7. Cook in the oven for about 50 minutes.

A COMFORTING
Cake

Prep Time: 10 mins
Total Time: 55 mins

Servings per Recipe: 24
Calories	155 kcal
Fat	6.4 g
Carbohydrates	24.3g
Protein	1.2 g
Cholesterol	11 mg
Sodium	171 mg

Ingredients

2 (16 oz.) cans peaches in heavy syrup
1 (18.25 oz.) package yellow cake mix
1/2 C. butter

1/2 tsp ground cinnamon, or to taste

Directions

1. Set your oven to 375 degrees F before doing anything else.
2. In the bottom of a 13x9-inch pan, place the peaches.
3. Spread the dry cake mix over the peaches and press down firmly.
4. Cut butter into small pieces and place on top of cake mix and sprinkle with the cinnamon evenly.
5. Cook in the oven for about 45 minutes.

Old-Fashioned
Cake

Prep Time: 40 mins
Total Time: 1 hr 20 mins

Servings per Recipe: 24
Calories	282 kcal
Fat	15.7 g
Carbohydrates	34.1g
Protein	2.8 g
Cholesterol	31 mg
Sodium	275 mg

Ingredients

1 (18.25 oz.) package yellow cake mix
1 (3.4 oz.) package instant vanilla pudding mix
1 (3.4 oz.) package instant butterscotch pudding mix
4 eggs

1 C. water
1 C. vegetable oil
1 C. packed brown sugar
1 tbsp ground cinnamon
1 C. chopped walnuts

Directions

1. Set your oven to 350 degrees F before doing anything else and grease a 10-inch bundt pan.
2. In a bowl, mix together the cake mix, butterscotch pudding mix and vanilla pudding mix.
3. Add the eggs, oil and water and mix till well combined.
4. In another bowl, mix together the brown sugar, cinnamon and walnuts.
5. Place half of the cake mix mixture into the pan evenly and top with the half of the walnut mixture.
6. Now, place the remaining cake mix mixture and top with the remaining walnut mixture.
7. Cook in the oven for about 20 minutes.
8. Now, set the oven to 325 degrees F and cook the cake for about 35-40 minutes more.

STRAWBERRY
Punch Cake

Prep Time: 15 mins
Total Time: 1 hr 20 mins

Servings per Recipe: 12
Calories	290 kcal
Fat	5 g
Carbohydrates	58.3g
Protein	3.1 g
Cholesterol	1 mg
Sodium	331 mg

Ingredients

2 C. crushed fresh strawberries
1 (6 oz.) package strawberry flavored
Jell-O(R) mix
3 C. miniature marshmallows

1 (18 oz.) package yellow cake mix, batter prepared as directed on package

Directions

1. Set your oven to 350 degrees F before doing anything else.
2. In the bottom of a 13x9-inch baking dish, spread the crushed strawberries and sprinkle with the dry gelatin powder and then top with the mini marshmallows.
3. Mix the cake mix according to the package's directions.
4. Transfer the mixture into the pan over the marshmallows and cook in the oven for about 40-50 minutes or till a toothpick inserted in the center comes out clean.

Gift Cake

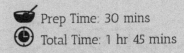
Prep Time: 30 mins
Total Time: 1 hr 45 mins

Servings per Recipe: 24
Calories   251 kcal
Fat   12.3 g
Carbohydrates   33.6g
Protein   2.4 g
Cholesterol   36 mg
Sodium   161 mg

Ingredients

1 (18.25 oz.) package yellow cake mix
3/4 C. vegetable oil
4 eggs
1 (8 oz.) container sour cream
1 C. brown sugar
1 tbsp ground cinnamon

2 C. confectioners' sugar
4 tbsp milk
1 tbsp vanilla extract

Directions

1. Set your oven to 325 degrees F before doing anything else.
2. In a large bowl, add the cake mix, sour cream, eggs and oil and beat till most the large lumps are gone.
3. Transfer half of the mixture into an ungreased 13x9-inch glass baking dish evenly.
4. In a small bowl, mix together the brown sugar and cinnamon and sprinkle over the cake mixture evenly.
5. Top with the remaining cake mix evenly and with a knife, twirl the cake till it looks like a honey bun.
6. Cook in the oven for about 40 minutes or till a toothpick inserted in the center comes out clean.
7. Meanwhile for frosting in a small bowl, add the confectioner's sugar, milk and vanilla and beat till smooth.
8. Spread the frosting over hot cake and serve warm.

CHOCOLATE
Coffee Cake

Prep Time: 20 mins
Total Time: 55 mins

Servings per Recipe: 12
Calories	320 kcal
Fat	11.3 g
Carbohydrates	53.2g
Protein	4.9 g
Cholesterol	33 mg
Sodium	359 mg

Ingredients

2 C. all-purpose flour
2 C. white sugar
3/4 C. unsweetened cocoa
2 tsp baking soda
1 tsp baking powder
1/2 tsp salt
2 eggs

1 C. cold brewed coffee
1 C. milk
1/2 C. vegetable oil
2 tsp vinegar

Directions

1. Set your oven to 350 degrees F before doing anything else and grease and flour a 13x9-inch cake pan.
2. In a large bowl, mix together the flour, cocoa powder, sugar, baking powder, baking soda and salt.
3. Make a well in the center of the mixture.
4. Add the eggs, coffee, milk, oil and vinegar and mix till smooth.
5. Transfer the mixture into the prepared pan and cook in the oven for about 35-40 minutes or till a toothpick inserted in the center comes out clean.

German Style Chocolate Cake

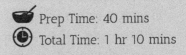 Prep Time: 40 mins

Total Time: 1 hr 10 mins

Servings per Recipe: 24

Calories	430 kcal
Fat	25.4 g
Carbohydrates	48.1g
Protein	5.2 g
Cholesterol	109 mg
Sodium	239 mg

Ingredients

4 (1 oz.) squares German sweet chocolate
1/2 C. water
2 C. all-purpose flour
1 tsp baking soda
1/4 tsp salt
1 C. butter, softened
2 C. white sugar
4 egg yolks
1 tsp vanilla extract
1 C. buttermilk
4 egg whites
12 fluid oz. evaporated milk

1 1/2 C. white sugar
3/4 C. butter
4 egg yolks
1 1/2 tsp vanilla extract
1 (8 oz.) package flaked coconut
1 1/2 C. chopped pecans

Directions

1. Set your oven to 350 degrees F before doing anything else and line a 13x9-inch pan with the parchment paper.
2. In a microwave safe bowl, add the chocolate and water and microwave on high for about 1 1/2 to 2 minutes, stirring once in the middle way.
3. In a medium bowl, mix together the flour, baking soda and salt.
4. In another large bowl, add 1 C. of the butter and 2 C. of the sugar and beat till fluffy and light.
5. Add 4 egg yolks one at a time, beating continuously.
6. Stir in the chocolate and 1 tsp of the vanilla extract.
7. Slowly, add the flour mixture alternately with the buttermilk, beating continuously till smooth.
8. In a third bowl, add the egg whites and beat on high till the soft peaks form.

9. Gently fold into the flour mixture.

10. Transfer the mixture into the prepared pan and cook in the oven for about 30 minutes or till a toothpick inserted in the center comes out clean.

11. For frosting in a large pan, mix together the milk, 1 1/2 C. of the sugar, 3/4 C. of the butter, 4 egg yolks and 1 1/2 tsp of the vanilla on medium heat and cook, stirring for about 12 minutes.

12. Remove from the heat and stir in the coconut and pecans.

13. Keep aside in the room temperature to cool.

Buttermilk
Chocolate Cake

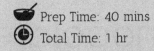 Prep Time: 40 mins

Total Time: 1 hr

Servings per Recipe: 14

Calories	684 kcal
Fat	35.4 g
Carbohydrates	87.1g
Protein	11.6 g
Cholesterol	80 mg
Sodium	393 mg

Ingredients

2 C. all-purpose flour
2 C. white sugar
1 tsp baking soda
1 C. butter
1/2 C. unsweetened cocoa powder
1 C. buttermilk
2 eggs, beaten
1 tsp vanilla extract

1 1/2 C. creamy peanut butter
1/2 C. butter
1/4 C. unsweetened cocoa powder
1/3 C. buttermilk
4 C. sifted confectioners' sugar
1 tsp vanilla extract

Directions

1. Set your oven to 350 degrees F before doing anything else and grease and flour a 13x9-inch baking pan.
2. In a large bowl, mix together flour, white sugar and baking soda.
3. In a heavy pan, melt 1 C. of the butter on medium heat and stir in 1/2 C. of the cocoa powder. Add the buttermilk and eggs and stir till well combined.
4. Bring to a boil, stirring continuously. Remove from the heat and stir in the flour mixture, stirring till smooth. Stir in 1 tsp of the vanilla.
5. Transfer the mixture into the prepared baking pan and cook in the oven for about 20-25 minutes or till a toothpick inserted in the center comes out clean.
6. Cool for about 10 minutes on a wire rack.
7. Carefully spread peanut butter over warm cake and let it cool completely.
8. For frosting in a small pan, mix together 1/2 C. of the butter, 1/4 C. of the cocoa powder and buttermilk on medium heat and bring to a boil, stirring continuously.
9. Place the mixture over the confectioners' sugar, stirring till smooth.
10. Stir in 1 tsp of the vanilla.
11. Spread chocolate frosting over peanut butter on cake.

SEMI-SWEET
Chocolate Cake

Prep Time: 15 mins
Total Time: 1 hr 55 mins

Servings per Recipe: 8
Calories   285 kcal
Fat   18.6 g
Carbohydrates   29.9g
Protein   4.5 g
Cholesterol   100 mg
Sodium   109 mg

Ingredients

4 (1 oz.) squares semisweet chocolate, chopped
1/2 C. butter
3/4 C. white sugar
1/2 C. cocoa powder

3 eggs, beaten
1 tsp vanilla extract

Directions

1. Set your oven to 300 degrees F before doing anything else and grease an 8-inch round cake pan and dust with the cocoa powder.
2. In the top of a double boiler over lightly simmering water, melt the chocolate and butter.
3. Remove from the heat and stir in the sugar, cocoa powder, eggs and vanilla.
4. Transfer the mixture into the prepared pan and cook in the oven for about 30 minutes.
5. Let the cake cool in the pan for about 10 minutes, then turn out onto a wire rack and cool completely.

Cookout Cake

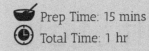

Prep Time: 15 mins
Total Time: 1 hr

Servings per Recipe: 24
Calories	155 kcal
Fat	5.5 g
Carbohydrates	25.7g
Protein	2.3 g
Cholesterol	16 mg
Sodium	240 mg

Ingredients

1 3/4 C. all-purpose flour
2 C. white sugar
3/4 C. unsweetened cocoa powder
2 tsp baking soda
1 tsp baking powder
1 tsp salt
2 eggs
1 C. strong brewed coffee

1 C. buttermilk
1/2 C. vegetable oil
1 tsp vanilla extract

Directions

1. Set your oven to 350 degrees F before doing anything else and grease 2 (9-inch) cake pans.
2. In large bowl mix together the flour, sugar, cocoa powder, baking soda, baking powder and salt.
3. Make a well in the center of the mixture.
4. Add the eggs, coffee, buttermilk, oil and vanilla and with an electric mixer, beat for 2 minutes on medium speed.
5. Transfer the mixture into the prepared pans and cook in the oven for about 30-40 minutes or till a toothpick inserted in the center comes out clean.
6. Remove from pans and finish cooling on a wire rack.
7. Fill and frost as desired.

NUTTY
Puff Sticks

🥣 Prep Time: 15 mins
🕐 Total Time: 30 mins

Servings per Recipe: 36
Calories	82 kcal
Fat	5.7 g
Carbohydrates	6.5g
Protein	1.3 g
Cholesterol	0 mg
Sodium	52 mg

Ingredients

1/2 C. Parmesan cheese
1 (17.5 oz) package frozen puff pastry, thawed
1 egg white, beaten

1/3 C. finely chopped shelled pistachios
kosher salt to taste

Directions

1. Before you do anything preheat the oven to 350 F.
2. Roll out the pastry sheets on a floured surface. Spread the egg white over them. Top them with some the pistachios and some kosher salt.
3. Flip the pastry sheet and repeat the process on the other side. Slice them into 3 inches long and 3/4 inches wide strips. Twist them gently and place them on lined baking sheet.
4. Cook them in the oven for 16 min. Allow them to cool down completely. Serve them with your favorite dip or dessert.
5. Enjoy.

Cheesy Mushroom Puffs

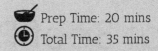

Prep Time: 20 mins
Total Time: 35 mins

Servings per Recipe: 2
Calories   630 kcal
Fat   50.9 g
Carbohydrates   31.1g
Protein   14.2 g
Cholesterol   73 mg
Sodium   458 mg

Ingredients

1/2 sheet puff pastry
3 tbsp butter
1/4 lb mushrooms, sliced
2 cloves garlic, crushed
1/2 C. crumbled goat cheese

4 tsp finely chopped fresh parsley

Directions

1. Before you do anything preheat the oven to 400 F. Coat a baking sheet with a cooking spray and place it aside.
2. Roll the pastry over a floured surface and slice it into 8 squares. Pierce the squares several times with a fork. Transfer them to the baking tray.
3. Cook them in the oven for 8 min. Press the squares with the back of a metal spatula. Cook them for 7 min in the oven again.
4. Place a pan over medium heat. Heat the butter in it. Add the garlic with mushroom, a pinch of salt and pepper. Cook them for 6 min.
5. Spoon the mix over the puff squares and top them with the goat cheese and parsley. Serve them.
6. Enjoy.

FANCY
Flat Beef Pies

Prep Time: 35 mins
Total Time: 1 hr 55 mins

Servings per Recipe: 2

Calories	3274 kcal
Fat	215.3 g
Carbohydrates	232.4g
Protein	68.7 g
Cholesterol	196 mg
Sodium	1359 mg

Ingredients

1 tsp olive oil
2 (6 oz) beef tenderloin filets
1 tbsp butter
8 oz fresh white mushrooms, minced
1/3 C. minced shallot
2 cloves garlic, minced
2 tbsp red wine

4 6-inch squares of frozen puff pastry,
thawed but still cold
1 1/2 C. red wine
salt and pepper to taste
1 egg (optional)
2 tbsp milk (optional)

Directions

1. Place a heavy pan over medium heat. Heat the oil in it. Add the beef fillets and cook them for 3 min on each side. Place them in the oven for 1 h.
2. Heat the butter in the same pan. Cook in it the mushrooms, shallot, and garlic for 7 min. Add 2 tbsp of red wine and stir them to scrap the brown bites.
3. Pour the mix in a bowl and place it in the fridge for 48 min.
4. Roll two pastry sheets on a floured working surface. Place a beef fillet over each one and top them with the cooked mushroom mix.
5. Cover them with a second sheet of pastry. Wet your fingers and seal the edges of the pastry. Use a sharp knife to make 2 slits on each beef packet.
6. Place a heavy saucepan over medium heat. Pour in it 1 1/2 C. of red wine. Cook it for 16 min until it reduces by half. Stir in the some salt and pepper to make the sauce.
7. Before you do anything preheat the oven to 450 F. Coat a baking sheet with a cooking spray and place it aside.
8. Get a mixing bowl: Mix in the milk with egg. Use a brush to spread the mix over the beef packets. Transfer them to the baking sheet.
9. Cook them in the oven for 16 min. Sere them warm with the wine sauce.
10. Enjoy.

Curried
Veggie Pot Pie

Prep Time: 20 mins
Total Time: 1 hr

Servings per Recipe: 8

Calories	518 kcal
Fat	31.6 g
Carbohydrates	52.5g
Protein	7.4 g
Cholesterol	13 mg
Sodium	356 mg

Ingredients

1 3/4 C. sweet potato, peeled and cut into 2-inch chunks
1 3/4 C. red potatoes, peeled and cut into 2-inch chunks
1 3/4 C. parsnips, peeled and cut into 2-inch chunks
1 3/4 C. carrots, peeled and cut into 2-inch chunks
2 tbsp olive oil
sea salt and ground black pepper to taste

1 tbsp butter
1 C. chopped onion
2 tbsp butter
1 1/2 C. vegetable broth
1/2 C. whole milk
3 tbsp all-purpose flour
1 1/2 tsp curry powder
1 (17.25 oz.) package frozen puff pastry, thawed and cut into four 5-inch squares

Directions

1. Set your oven to 400 degrees F before doing anything else.
2. In a roasting pan, add the sweet potato, red potatoes, parsnips, carrots, olive oil, sea salt and black pepper and toss to coat well.
3. Cook in the oven for about 20-30 minutes.
4. In a pan, melt 1 tbsp of the butter on medium heat and cook the onion for about 3-5 minutes.
5. Add the sweet potato mixture, 2 tbsp of the butter, salt and black pepper and cook for about 2-3 minutes.
6. In another pan, heat the vegetable broth and milk on medium heat,
7. Stir in the flour and curry powder till well combined.
8. Slowly, add the broth mixture and cook for about 3 minutes, stirring continuously.
9. Divide mixture into 4 pot pie dishes and top each with a puff pastry square.
10. Cook in the oven for about 17-20 minutes.

OLD-FASHIONED
Turkey Pot Pie

Prep Time: 45 mins
Total Time: 1 hr 25 mins

Servings per Recipe: 8
Calories	502 kcal
Fat	31.6 g
Carbohydrates	39.6g
Protein	16 g
Cholesterol	69 mg
Sodium	868 mg

Ingredients

2 C. all-purpose flour
1 tsp salt
7 tbsp cold vegetable shortening
6 tbsp cold butter
6 tbsp cold water
3 tbsp butter
2 carrots, diced
1 onion, diced
2 stalks celery, diced
1/8 tsp ground black pepper
2 tbsp all-purpose flour

2 C. cubed cooked turkey
2 tbsp butter
2 C. chicken broth
1 (15 oz.) can cut green beans, drained
1 (10.75 oz.) can condensed cream of mushroom soup
1/2 (15 oz.) can cream-style corn
1 tbsp chopped fresh flat-leaf parsley
1 tbsp chopped fresh thyme

Directions

1. In a bowl, mix together 2 C. of the flour and salt.
2. With a pastry cutter, cut in the vegetable shortening and 6 tbsp of the cold butter till the butter and shortening are the size of small peas.
3. Sprinkle with the cold water, 1 tbsp at a time and with a fork gently, mix till anon-sticky dough is formed.
4. Divide the dough into 2 equal-sized pieces and shape each into a round.
5. Refrigerate till using.
6. Set your oven to 425 degrees F.
7. In a large skillet, melt 3 tbsp of the butter on medium heat and cook the carrots, onion, celery and black pepper for about 8 minutes.
8. Transfer the mixture into a bowl and keep aside.
9. In a resealable plastic zipper bag, place 2 tbsp of flour and cooked turkey meat.
10. Seal the bag and shake the to coat.

11. In the same skillet, melt 2 tbsp of the butter on medium heat and cook the turkey meat for about 10 minutes.
12. Add the chicken broth, 1/2 C. at a time and bring to a simmer, stirring occasionally.
13. Cook for about 5 minutes, stirring occasionally.
14. Remove from the heat and stir in the cooked vegetables, green beans, cream of mushroom soup, cream-style corn, parsley and thyme till well combined.
15. Place each dough piece onto a floured surface and roll into a 11-inch circle.
16. Place the crust into a 10-inch pie dish and press to fit.
17. Place the filling into the bottom of crust and cover with the second crust.
18. Pinch the edges to seal the filling.
19. Cut 5 slits into the top crust.
20. Cook in the oven for about 15 minutes.
21. Now, set your oven to 350 degrees F and cook for about 25 minutes more

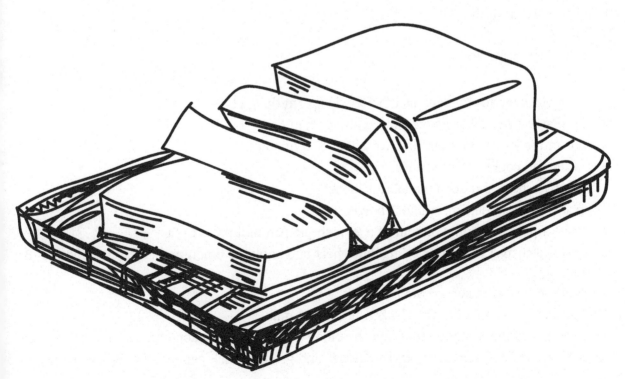

SEAFOOD
Sampler Pot Pie

Prep Time: 15 mins
Total Time: 1 hr 25 mins

Servings per Recipe: 6	
Calories	587 kcal
Fat	33.1 g
Carbohydrates	46.7g
Protein	25.8 g
Cholesterol	119 mg
Sodium	1058 mg

Ingredients

1 (3 oz.) package dry crab boil
5 small lobster tails
1 (15 oz.) package double crust ready-to-use pie crust
5 tbsp butter
1/2 C. diced onion
1/2 C. diced celery
1/3 C. all-purpose flour
1 1/2 C. chicken broth
3/4 C. milk
1 tsp seafood seasoning

1/2 tsp garlic powder
1/4 tsp freshly ground black pepper
1 1/2 C. frozen mixed vegetables, thawed
1/2 C. diced potato

Directions

1. Set your oven to 425 degrees F before doing anything else.
2. In a large pan, add the water and crab boil and bring to a boil.
3. Stir in the lobster tails and boil for about 5-8 minutes.
4. Drain and cool the lobster tails.
5. Remove shells and chop the lobster meat.
6. Transfer the lobster meat into a bowl.
7. Place a pie crust in the bottom of a 9-inch pie pan and press to fit.
8. In a skillet, melt the butter on medium heat and cook the onion and celery for about 5-8 minutes.
9. Add the flour and stir to combine well.
10. In a bowl, mix together the chicken broth and milk.
11. Slowly, add the broth mixture into the onion mixture, stirring continuously till thickened.
12. Add the seafood seasoning, garlic powder and ground black pepper and stir to combine

well.

13. Stir in the thawed vegetables, diced potato and cooked lobster meat and simmer for about 8 minutes.

14. Place the lobster mixture into the prepared pie crust and cover with the remaining pie crust.

15. Crimping the edges to seal the filling.

16. With a sharp knife, cut an 'X' into top of pie crust.

17. Cook in the oven for about 40 - 45 minutes.

18. Remove from the oven and keep aside to cool for about 10 - 15 minutes before serving.

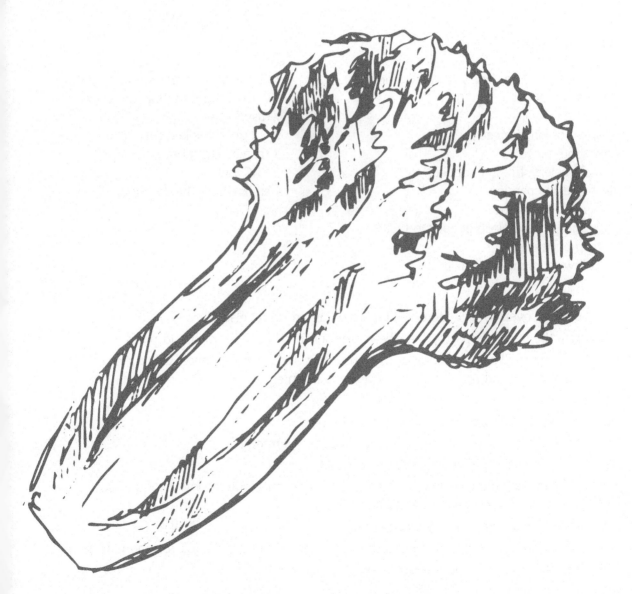

NOVEMBER'S
Pot Pie

Prep Time: 20 mins
Total Time: 1 hr 40 mins

Servings per Recipe: 6

Calories	563 kcal
Fat	32.4 g
Carbohydrates	45.9 g
Protein	21.7 g
Cholesterol	52 mg
Sodium	513 mg

Ingredients

1 (15 oz.) package pastry for a 10-inch double crust pie
2 tsp canola oil
1 small onion, minced
2 carrots, diced
1 stalk celery, finely chopped
2 tbsp dried parsley
1 tsp dried oregano
salt and ground black pepper to taste
1 tbsp butter
2 C. low-sodium chicken broth

1 C. peeled and cubed sweet potato
1 C. frozen green peas
1 tbsp butter
2 C. cubed cooked turkey
3 tbsp all-purpose flour
2/3 C. milk
1 stalk celery, finely chopped

Directions

1. Set your oven to 425 degrees F before doing anything else.
2. Place the pie crust pastry into the bottom of a 10-inch pie dish and press to fit.
3. In a large skillet, heat the oil on medium heat and cook the onion, carrots, celery, parsley, oregano, salt and black pepper for about 5 minutes.
4. Stir in 1 tbsp of the butter till melted.
5. Add the chicken broth and bring to a boil.
6. Stir in the sweet potato and simmer for about 15 minutes.
7. Stir in the peas and reduce the heat to low.
8. In a pan, melt the remaining 1 tbsp of the butter on medium-low heat and cook the turkey and flour for about 5 minutes.
9. Add the milk and bring to a gentle boil.
10. Transfer the turkey mixture into the vegetable mixture and cook for about 10 minutes.
11. Remove from the heat and keep aside to cool.

12. Cook the bottom crust in the oven for about 8 minutes.

13. Remove from the oven and keep aside to cool for about 5 minutes.

14. Place the turkey mixture into crust and cover with the remaining crust.

15. Pinch the edges to seal the filling.

16. Cut four slits in the top crust.

17. Cook in the oven for about 15 minutes.

18. Now, set your oven to 350 degrees F and cook for about 10 minutes more.

TURKEY
& Potato Pot Pie

Prep Time: 20 mins
Total Time: 1 hr 10 mins

Servings per Recipe: 12

CCalories	490 kcal
Fat	27 g
Carbohydrates	40.1g
Protein	20.3 g
Cholesterol	40 mg
Sodium	782 mg

Ingredients

1 tbsp olive oil
1 3/4 C. diced onions
1 tsp minced garlic
1 (26 oz.) can cream of chicken soup
1/4 C. white wine
2 tsp ground black pepper
1 tsp herbes de Provence
1 tsp poultry seasoning
1/2 tsp dried oregano

1/4 tsp dried basil
salt to taste
4 C. cubed cooked turkey
1 1/4 C. diced potatoes
1 C. frozen peas
1 C. diced carrots

Directions

1. Set your oven to 425 degrees F before doing anything else.
2. In a deep skillet, heat the oil on medium heat and cook the onions and garlic for about 5 minutes.
3. Add the cream of chicken soup, wine, black pepper, herbes de Provence, poultry seasoning, oregano, basil and salt and bring to a simmer.
4. Remove from the heat and gently, stir in the turkey, potatoes, peas and carrots.
5. Place 2 pie crusts into two 9-inch pie dishes and press to fit.
6. Place the filling into the pie crusts evenly and top each with a second pie crust.
7. Pinch the edges to seal the filling.
8. Cut several slits in the top crust of each pie.
9. Cook in the oven for about 30-35 minutes.
10. Remove from the oven and keep aside to cool for about 10 minutes before serving.

Zesty
Italian Pot Pie

Prep Time: 20 mins
Total Time: 50 mins

Servings per Recipe: 6

Calories	283 kcal
Fat	12.5 g
Carbohydrates	24.8g
Protein	18.1 g
Cholesterol	39 mg
Sodium	449 mg

Ingredients

1 lb. boneless skinless chicken breasts, cut into bite-size pieces
1/4 C. KRAFT Lite Zesty Italian Dressing
4 oz. PHILADELPHIA Neufchatel cheese, cubed
2 tbsp flour
1/2 C. fat-free reduced-sodium chicken broth

3 C. frozen mixed vegetables (peas, carrots, corn, green beans), thawed, drained
1/2 (15 oz.) package ready-to-use refrigerated pie crust

Directions

1. Set your oven to 375 degrees F before doing anything else.
2. Heat a large skillet on medium heat and cook the chicken in dressing for about 2 minutes.
3. Add the Neufchatel and cook for about 3-5 minutes.
4. Stir in the flour till well combined.
5. Stir in the broth and vegetables and simmer for about 5 minutes.
6. Place the mixture into a 10-inch deep-dish pie plate and cover with a pie crust.
7. Crimp and flute the edge.
8. Cut slits in top crust.
9. Cook in the oven for about 30 minute

AMERICAN
Chicken Pot Pie

Prep Time: 5 mins
Total Time: 35 mins

Servings per Recipe: 6
Calories   209 kcal
Fat   8 g
Carbohydrates   22g
Protein   12.4 g
Cholesterol   57 mg
Sodium   622 mg

Ingredients

1 2/3 C. frozen mixed vegetables
1 C. cut-up cooked chicken
1 (10.75 oz.) can condensed cream of
chicken soup

1 C. Bisquick mix
1/2 C. milk
1 egg

Directions

1. Set your oven to 400 degrees F before doing anything else.
2. In an 9x1-1/4-inch ungreased glass pie plate, mix together the vegetables, chicken and soup.
3. In a bowl, add the remaining ingredients and with a fork, mix till well combined.
4. Place the mixture into pie plate and cook in the oven for about 30 minutes.

Chicken
& Corn Pot Pie

Prep Time: 10 mins
Total Time: 55 mins

Servings per Recipe: 6

Calories	469 kcal
Fat	24.5 g
Carbohydrates	48g
Protein	13.9 g
Cholesterol	40 mg
Sodium	458 mg

Ingredients

1 (15 oz.) box refrigerated pie crusts, softened as directed on box
1 (9 oz.) pouch creamy roasted garlic with chicken stock cooking sauce
1/4 C. all-purpose flour
1/2 tsp poultry seasoning

1 (12 oz.) bag frozen mixed vegetables, thawed and drained
1 1/2 C. chopped deli rotisserie chicken

Directions

1. Set your oven to 425 degrees F before doing anything else.
2. Prepare the pie crusts according to box's directions for Two-Crust Pie.
3. Place a crust into 9-inch glass pie plate and press to fit.
4. In a bowl, add the cooking sauce, poultry seasoning, 1/2 tsp of the salt and 1/4 tsp of the pepper and mix till smooth.
5. Add the chicken and vegetables and stir to combine.
6. Place the filling mixture into the bottom crust and cover with the second crust.
7. Crimp the edges and flute.
8. Cut several slits in the top crust.
9. Cook in the oven for about 20 minutes.
10. Now, cover the edge of crust with strips of foil and cook in the oven for about 10 minutes.
11. Remove from the oven and keep aside to cool for about 10 minutes before serving

A QUICHE
Of Mushrooms and Spinach

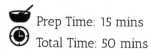

Prep Time: 15 mins
Total Time: 50 mins

Servings per Recipe: 9
Calories   325 kcal
Carbohydrates   10.8 g
Cholesterol   139 mg
Fat   22.5 g
Protein   20.9 g
Sodium   806 mg

Ingredients

6 slices turkey bacon
4 eggs, beaten
1 1/2 cups light cream
1/4 tsp ground nutmeg
1/2 tsp salt
1/2 tsp pepper
2 cups chopped fresh spinach

2 cups chopped fresh mushrooms
1/2 cup chopped onions
1 cup shredded Swiss cheese
1 cup shredded Cheddar cheese
1 (9 inch) deep dish pie crust

Directions

1. Preheat your oven at 400 degrees F and put some oil over the quiche dish.
2. Cook bacon over medium heat until brown and then crumble it after draining.
3. Mix eggs, pepper, cream, salt, nutmeg, bacon, spinach, mushrooms, 3/4 cup Swiss cheese, 3/4 cup Cheddar cheese and onions in a bowl very thoroughly.
4. Pour this mixture over the pie crust and add some cheese.
5. Bake in the preheated oven for about 35 minutes or until the top of the quiche is golden brown in color.

Sweet
French Bread Soufflé

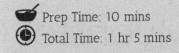 Prep Time: 10 mins

Total Time: 1 hr 5 mins

Servings per Recipe: 12

Calories	811.5
Fat	29.0g
Cholesterol	249.5mg
Sodium	1101.2mg
Carbohydrates	108.9g
Protein	29.3g

Ingredients

1/2 C. butter, softened
8 oz. cream cheese
1/2 C. maple syrup
2 loaves French bread, cubed
12 eggs

3 C. half-and-half
1 1/2 tsp vanilla
ground cinnamon, for dusting
powdered sugar, for dusting

Directions

1. Grease 2 (7x11-inch) baking dishes with some butter.
2. Place bread cubes into prepared baking dishes about half way full.
3. In a small bowl, add the cream cheese, butter and maple syrup and mix until well combined.
4. In another large bowl, add the half-and-half, eggs and vanilla and beat until well combined.
5. Place the cream cheese mixture over bread cubes evenly, followed by the egg mixture.
6. Sprinkle with the cinnamon and refrigerate, covered overnight.
7. Set your oven to 350 degrees F.
8. Remove the baking dish from refrigerator and cook in the oven for about 55-60 minutes.
9. Remove from the oven and serve with a dusting of the powdered sugar.

SPINACH
Muenster Quiche

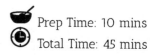

Prep Time: 10 mins
Total Time: 45 mins

Servings per Recipe: 8
Calories	311 kcal
Carbohydrates	4.5 g
Cholesterol	122 mg
Fat	25.4 g
Protein	17.8 g
Sodium	484 mg

Ingredients

8 ounces Muenster cheese, sliced
2 (10 ounce) packages frozen chopped
spinach, thawed and drained
2 eggs
1/3 cup grated Parmesan cheese
1 (8 ounce) package cream cheese,
softened

salt and pepper to taste
garlic powder to taste
4 ounces Muenster cheese, sliced

Directions

1. Preheat your oven to 350 degrees F and put some oil over the quiche dish.
2. Put Muenster cheese slices into the dish and then pour into it the mixture of spinach (all water drained), eggs, Parmesan cheese, cream cheese, salt, pepper and garlic powder.
3. Bake in the preheated oven for about 30 minutes or until the top of the quiche is golden brown in color.

American
Gratin Soufflé

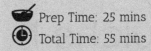 Prep Time: 25 mins
Total Time: 55 mins

Servings per Recipe: 4
Calories   297.7
Fat   18.5g
Cholesterol   127.7mg
Sodium   351.1mg
Carbohydrates   26.1g
Protein   8.2g

Ingredients

1 large eggplant, pared and cubed
2 beaten eggs
1/2 C. milk
1/2 C. dry breadcrumbs
1 C. shredded American cheese

1/4 C. melted butter
3/4 C. crushed crackers

Directions

1. Set your oven to 350 degrees F before doing anything else and grease a casserole dish.
2. In a pan of salted boiling water, cook the eggplant cubes for about 15 minutes.
3. Drain the eggplant cubes well and transfer into a a bowl.
4. With a fork, mash the eggplant cubes well.
5. Add the 3/4 C. of the cheese, milk, eggs, breadcrumbs, salt and pepper and mix until well combined.
6. In another small bowl, add the crackers and melted butter and mix well.
7. Place the eggplant mixture into the prepared casserole dish evenly and top with the cracker mixture, followed by the remaining 1/4 C. of the cheese.
8. Cook in the oven for about 30 minutes.

NEW ENGLAND
Quiche I

Prep Time: 10 mins
Total Time: 1 hr

Servings per Recipe: 6
Calories   326 kcal
Carbohydrates   14.3 g
Cholesterol   83 mg
Fat   24.8 g
Protein   11.8 g
Sodium   308 mg

Ingredients

1/2 cup mayonnaise
2 tbsps all-purpose flour
2 eggs, beaten
1/2 cup milk
1 cup crab meat

1 cup diced Swiss cheese
1/2 cup chopped green onions
1 (9 inch) unbaked pie crust

Directions

1. Preheat your oven at 350 degrees F and put some oil over the quiche dish.
2. Whisk eggs, milk, mayonnaise, crab, flour, onion and cheese very thoroughly.
3. Pour this mixture in the quiche dish.
4. Bake in the preheated oven for about 30 minutes or until the top of the quiche is golden brown in color.

Bittersweet
Soufflé

🥣 Prep Time: 15 mins
🕐 Total Time: 27 mins

Servings per Recipe: 12
Calories   216.4
Fat   17.7g
Cholesterol   133.6mg
Sodium   170.6mg
Carbohydrates   11.4g
Protein   3.5g

Ingredients

8 oz. bittersweet chocolate, chopped
8 oz. butter, diced
6 eggs
4 oz. sugar

1 oz. sifted flour
nonstick cooking spray

Directions

1. Set your oven to 325 degrees F before doing anything else and grease 12 soufflé dishes with non-stick spray.
2. In the top of a double boiler, place the chocolate and butter and heat until melted, stirring continuously.
3. In a bowl, add the eggs and sugar and beat until light and fluffy.
4. Add the flour into the bowl of chocolate mixture and mix well
5. Gently fold the chocolate mixture into the flour mixture.
6. Place the mixture into the prepared soufflé dishes evenly.
7. Cook in the oven for about 9 - 12 minutes.
8. Serve immediately.

DIARY
Dreams Quiche

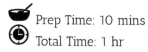

Prep Time: 10 mins
Total Time: 1 hr

Servings per Recipe: 6
Calories	462 kcal
Carbohydrates	20.2 g
Cholesterol	183 mg
Fat	31.5 g
Protein	24.7 g
Sodium	993 mg

Ingredients

1 (3 ounce) can turkey bacon bits
1/2 cup chopped onion
5 ounces shredded Swiss cheese
3 ounces grated Cheddar cheese
1 (9 inch pie) deep dish frozen pie crust

4 eggs, lightly beaten
1 cup half-and-half cream

Directions

1. Preheat your oven to 400 degrees F and put some oil over the quiche dish.

2. Pour mixture of eggs and half-and-half over the mixture of both cheeses, bacon and onion in the dish.

3. Bake in the preheated oven for about 15 minutes and then an additional 35 minutes at 350 degrees F or until the top of the quiche is golden brown in color.

Soufflé Mornings

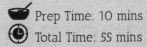 Prep Time: 10 mins

Total Time: 55 mins

Servings per Recipe: 6
Calories   445.3
Fat   29.2g
Cholesterol   297.9mg
Sodium   1168.3mg
Carbohydrates   17.2g
Protein   27.0g

Ingredients

1 lb. mild bulk beef sausage
6 eggs
2 C. milk
1 tsp salt

1 tsp dry mustard
6 slices white bread (cubed)
1 C. cheddar cheese (grated)

Directions

1. Heat a skillet and cook the crumbled sausage until browned.
2. Drain the grease and keep aside to cool.
3. In a large bowl, add the eggs, add milk, dry mustard and salt and beat well.
4. Add the bread cubes and stir to combine.
5. Add the cheese and browned sausage and mix well.
6. Refrigerate, covered overnight.
7. Set your oven to 350 degrees F.
8. Cook in the oven for about 45 minutes.

EASY
Cinnamon Rolls

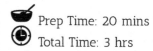

Prep Time: 20 mins
Total Time: 3 hrs

Servings per Recipe: 12
Calories	525 kcal
Fat	18.6 g
Carbohydrates	82g
Protein	9 g
Cholesterol	64 mg
Sodium	388 mg

Ingredients

1 C. warm milk (110 degrees F/45 degrees C)
2 eggs, room temperature
1/3 C. margarine, melted
4 1/2 C. bread flour
1 tsp salt
1/2 C. white sugar
2 1/2 tsps bread machine yeast
1 C. brown sugar, packed

2 1/2 tbsps ground cinnamon
1/3 C. butter, softened
1 (3 oz.) package cream cheese, softened
1/4 C. butter, softened
1 1/2 C. confectioners' sugar
1/2 tsp vanilla extract
1/8 tsp salt

Directions

1. Add all the ingredients to your bread machine except the cinnamon and sugar.
2. Set the bread machine to the dough cycle and let it work.
3. Once the dough has been formed knead it on a floured surface and let it sit in a bowl until it doubles in size.
4. Get a bowl, combine: cinnamon and brown sugar.
5. Now form a 16x21 inch rectangle.
6. Coat the dough with 1/3 C. of butter and then top it with the cinnamon mix.
7. Divide the dough into 12 pieces and shape each piece into a roll.
8. Layer the rolls on an oiled baking pan and place a covering on the pan.
9. Let the dough sit for 40 mins.
10. Now set your oven to 400 degrees and cook the rolls in oven for 20 mins in the oven once it is hot.
11. As the rolls cook get a bowl, combine: salt, cream cheese, vanilla, 1/4 C. butter, and confectioners. Coat your rolls with the cream cheese mix.
12. Enjoy.

Rolls
for Dinner-Time

Prep Time: 20 mins
Total Time: 2 hrs 20 mins

Servings per Recipe: 16

Calories	192 kcal
Fat	7.5 g
Carbohydrates	27.1g
Protein	3.9 g
Cholesterol	30 mg
Sodium	202 mg

Ingredients

1/2 C. warm water (110 degrees F/45 degrees C)
1/2 C. warm milk
1 egg
1/3 C. butter, softened
1/3 C. white sugar

1 tsp salt
3 3/4 C. all-purpose flour
1 (.25 oz.) package active dry yeast
1/4 C. butter, softened

Directions

1. Add the following to your bread machine: yeast, water, flour, milk, salt, egg, sugar, and 1/3 C. butter.
2. Set the machine to the dough / knead cycle to form a dough.
3. Once the dough is finished break it into two pieces and roll each piece into a 12 inch circle.
4. Coach each piece with 1/4 C. butter. Then slice each of the halves into 8 pieces.
5. Roll each of the 8 pieces tightly then layer everything on a baking sheet.
6. Place a kitchen towel covering over everything and let the dough sit for 60 mins.
7. Now set your oven to 400 degrees before doing anything else.
8. Once the oven is hot cook the bread in the oven for 12 mins.
9. Enjoy.

MAGGIE'S
Easy Pretzels

Prep Time: 2 hrs
Total Time: 2 hrs 20 mins

Servings per Recipe: 12
Calories	237 kcal
Fat	1.7 g
Carbohydrates	48.9g
Protein	5.9 g
Cholesterol	0 mg
Sodium	4681 mg

Ingredients

4 tsps active dry yeast
1 tsp white sugar
1 1/4 C. warm water (110 degrees F/45 degrees C)
5 C. all-purpose flour
1/2 C. white sugar

1 1/2 tsps salt
1 tbsp vegetable oil
1/2 C. baking soda
4 C. hot water
1/4 C. kosher salt, for topping

Directions

1. Get a bowl, combine: 1 1/4 C. warm water, yeast, 1 tsp sugar. Leave the mix for 12 mins.
2. Get a 2nd bigger bowl, combine: salt, flour, and half C. sugar. Combine in the oil and stir the mix until its smooth.
3. Now combine both bowls and make a dough.
4. Knead the mix for 10 mins and if the dough is too dry add a tbsp of water.
5. Get a 3rd bowl and coat it with oil then place the dough in the bowl and turn the dough to get it oily.
6. Place a covering of plastic around the bowl and let the dough sit for 60 mins.
7. Now set your oven to 450 degrees before doing anything else.
8. Coat two cookie sheets with oil.
9. Get a 4th big bowl and combine 4 C. of hot water and baking soda.
10. Now grab your dough and divide it into 12 pieces.
11. Roll each piece into a long rope then form it into a pretzel shape.
12. Now coat each pretzel with the baking soda mix then layer everything on your cookie sheets.
13. Top the dough with your kosher salt and cook everything in the oven for 10 mins.
14. Enjoy.

Parmesan Poppers

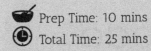

Prep Time: 10 mins
Total Time: 25 mins

Servings per Recipe: 8
Calories   157 kcal
Fat   9.5 g
Carbohydrates   15.3g
Protein   2.9 g
Cholesterol   13 mg
Sodium   400 mg

Ingredients

3 tbsps melted butter
1/4 tsp dill weed
1/4 tsp celery seed
1/4 tsp minced onion
1 tbsp grated Parmesan cheese

1 (10 oz.) can refrigerated biscuit dough, separated and cut into half circles
1 tbsp grated Parmesan cheese

Directions

1. Set your oven to 425 degrees before doing anything else.
2. Get a pie dish and add your melted butter to it.
3. Get a bowl, combine: 1 tbsp parmesan, dill, onion, and celery seed. Add this to the melted butter.
4. In the middle of your pie dish add one biscuit then layer your other biscuits around the first one.
5. Now add a topping of parmesan (1 tbsp) over everything.
6. Cook the mix in the oven for 17 mins.
7. Enjoy.

CRANBERRY
Bread

Prep Time: 15 mins
Total Time: 1 hr 5 mins

Servings per Recipe: 12
Calories	194
Fat	6.1g
Cholesterol	16mg
Sodium	265mg
Carbohydrates	32.1g
Protein	3.6g

Ingredients

2 C. all-purpose flour
½ tsp baking soda
1½ tsp baking powder
¾ tsp salt
1 egg
¾ C. white sugar

2 tbsp vegetable oil
¾ C. fresh orange juice
1 C. cranberries, chopped
½ C. walnuts, chopped
1 tbsp fresh orange zest, grated finely

Directions

1. Set your oven to 350 degrees F. Oil a bread pan.
2. In a large bowl, mix together flour, baking soda, baking powder and salt.
3. In another bowl, add egg, sugar, oil and orange juice and beat till well combined.
4. Add egg mixture into flour mixture and mix till well combined.
5. Fold in cranberries, walnuts and orange zest.
6. Transfer the mixture into prepared bread pan.
7. Bake for about 50 minutes or till a toothpick inserted in the center comes out clean.
8. Let the bread cool for 10 minutes before removing from pan.
9. Enjoy.

Easy
Portuguese Bread

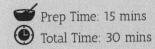 Prep Time: 15 mins

Total Time: 30 mins

Servings per Recipe: 16
Calories	118 kcal
Fat	5.9 g
Carbohydrates	14.3g
Protein	2 g
Cholesterol	< 1 mg
Sodium	< 169 mg

Ingredients

2 C. all-purpose flour
3 tsps baking powder
1/2 tsp salt
2 tbsps white sugar

3/4 C. milk
1 quart vegetable oil for frying

Directions

1. Get a bowl, combine: sugar, flour, salt, and baking powder.
2. Combine in the milk and stir the contents into a dough.
3. Shape the mix into small balls. Then flatten them on a working surface.
4. Each piece should have half an inch of thickness.
5. Now fry everything in hot oil until brown, then flip, and fry again.
6. Enjoy.

ENJOY THE RECIPES?
KEEP ON COOKING
WITH 6 MORE FREE COOKBOOKS!

Visit our website and simply enter your email address to join the club and receive your 6 cookbooks.

http://booksumo.com/magnet

https://www.instagram.com/booksumopress/

https://www.facebook.com/booksumo/

Made in United States
North Haven, CT
04 December 2021

11934493R00052